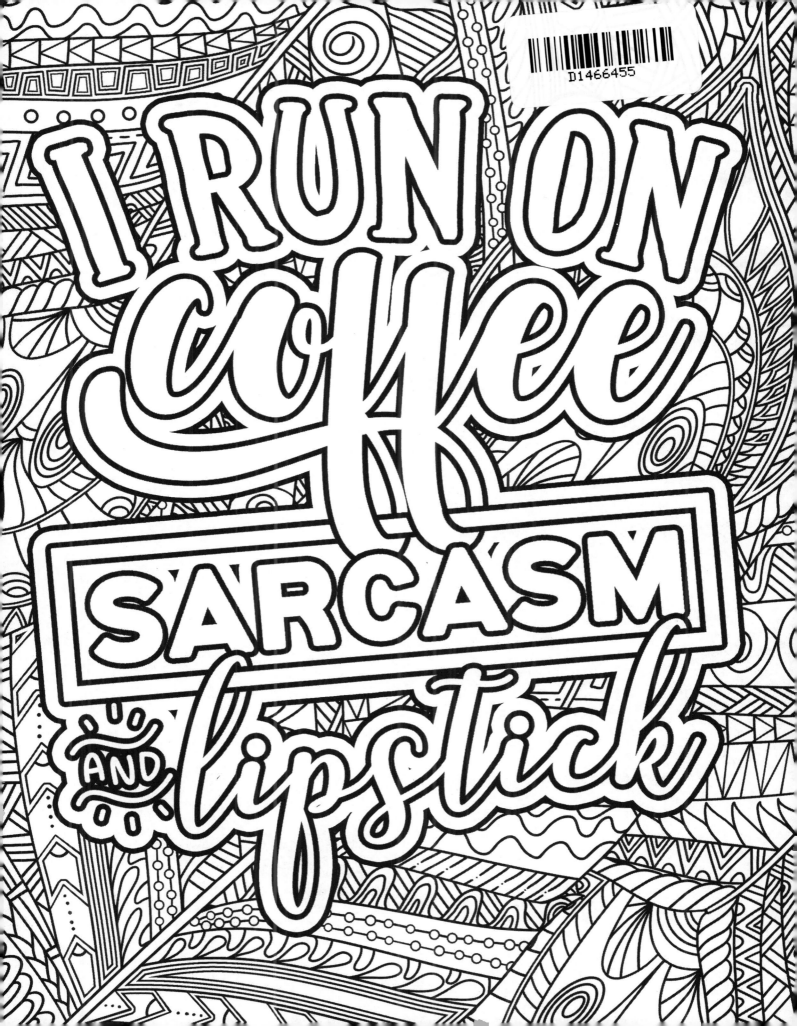

ISBN-13: 978-1-64001-070-3
ISBN-10: 1-64001-070-X

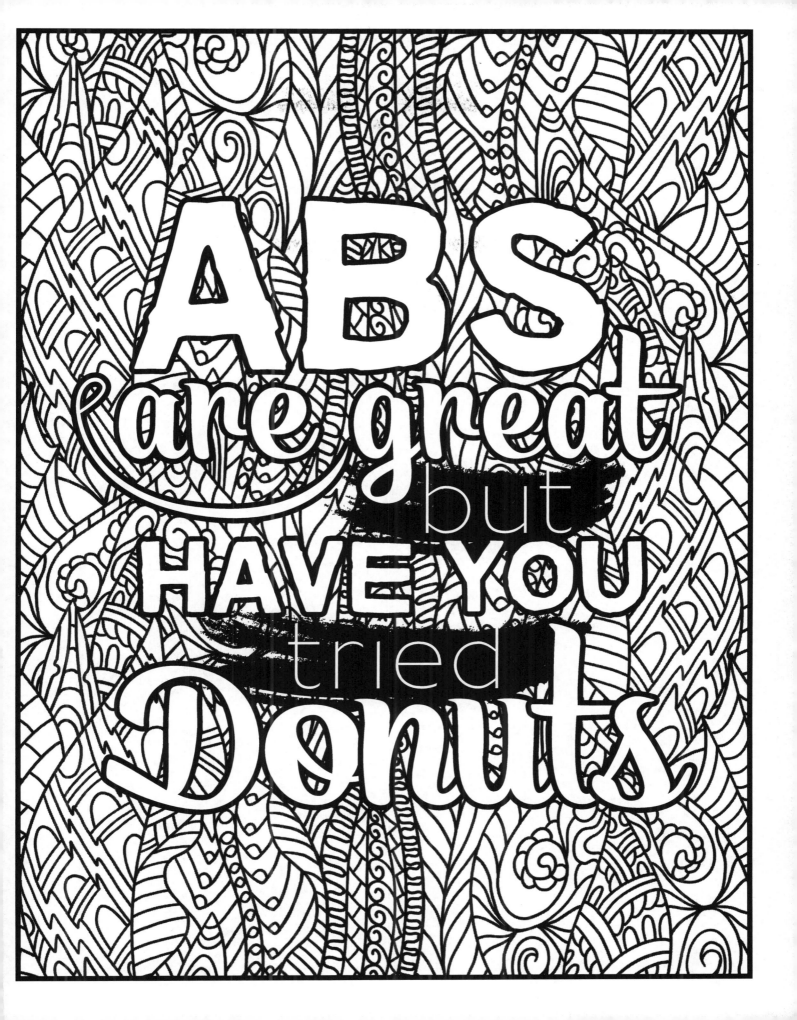

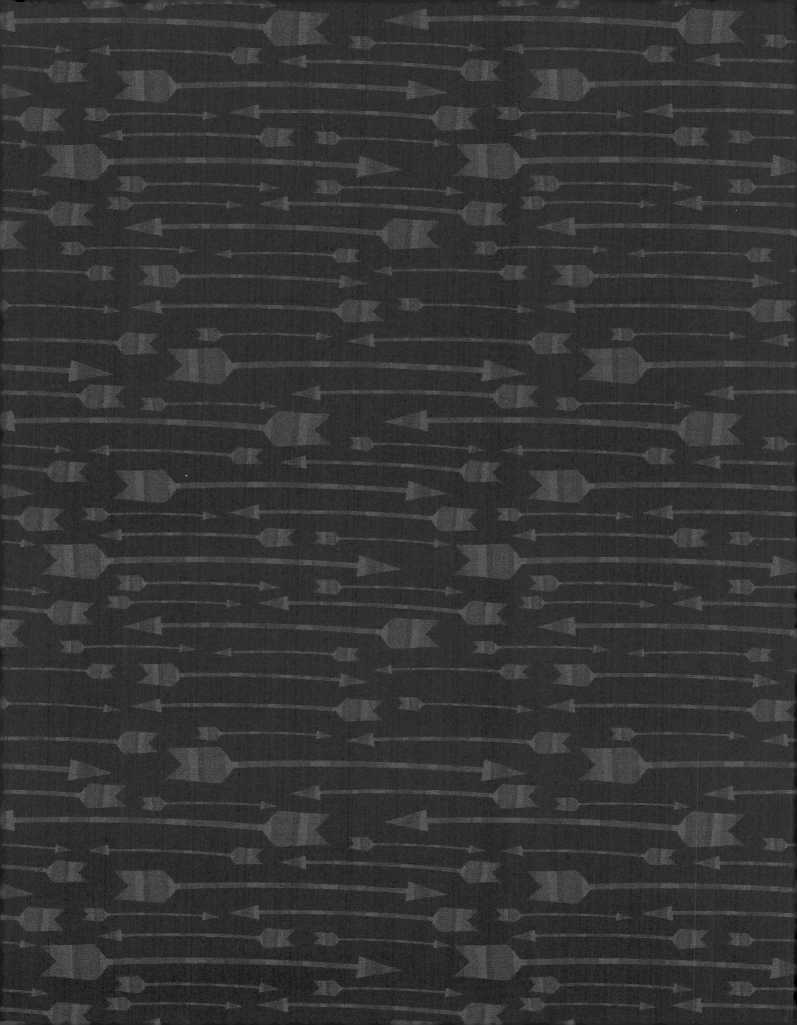

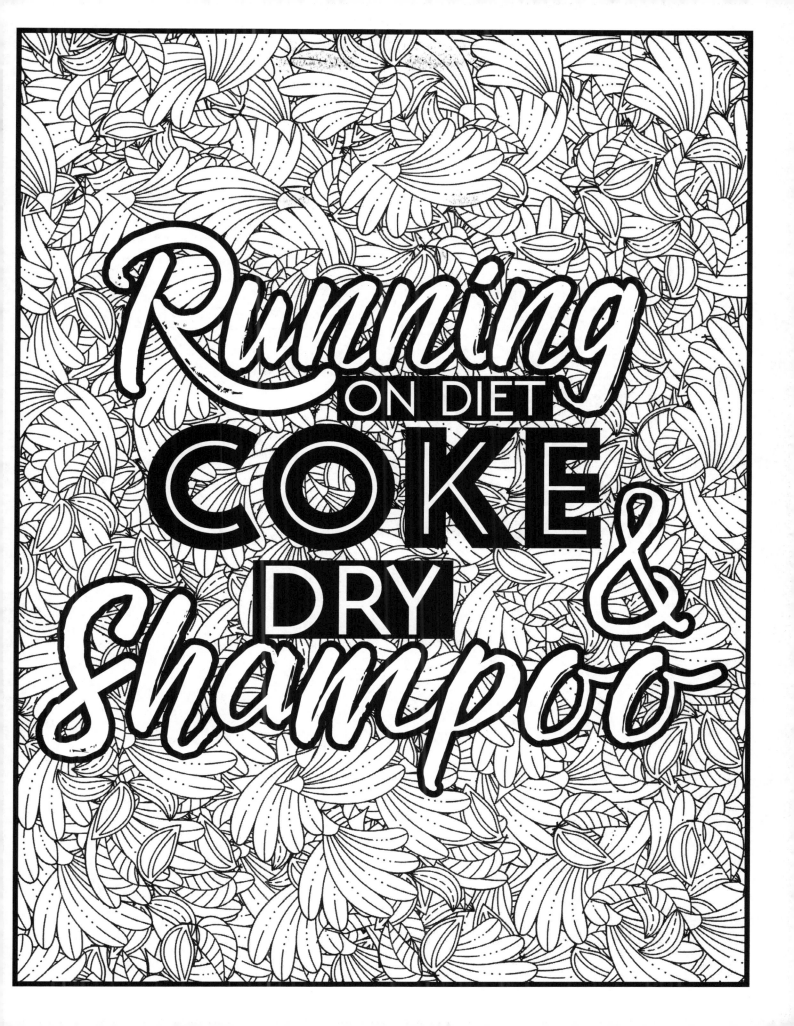

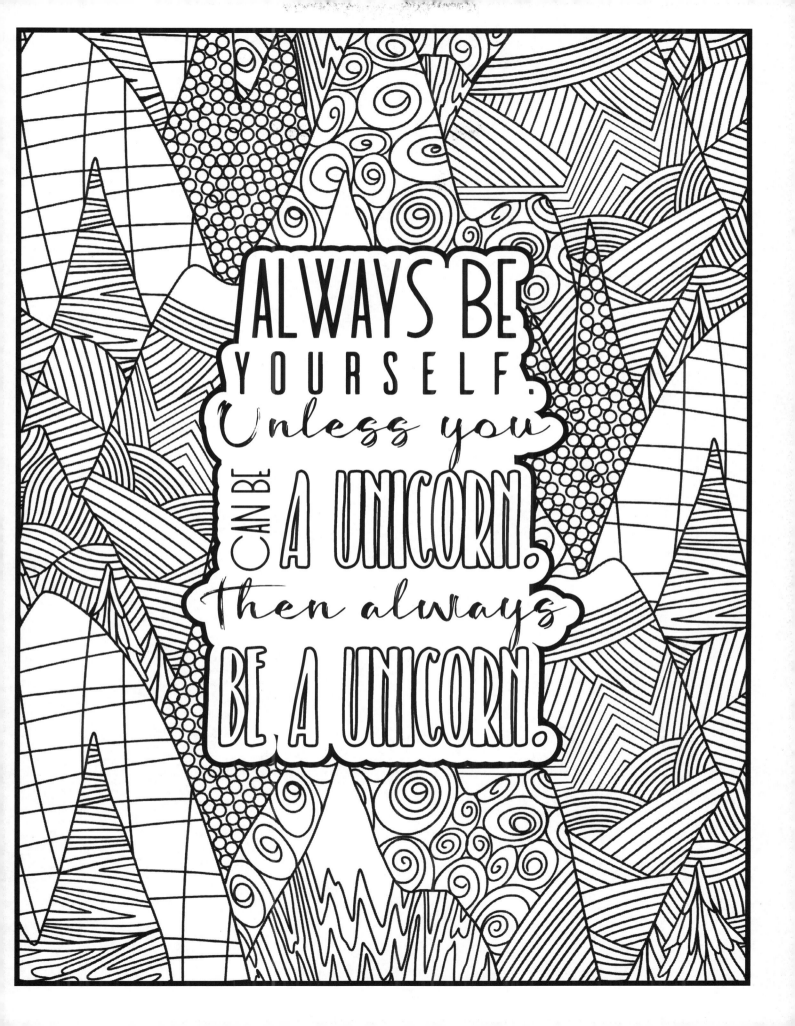

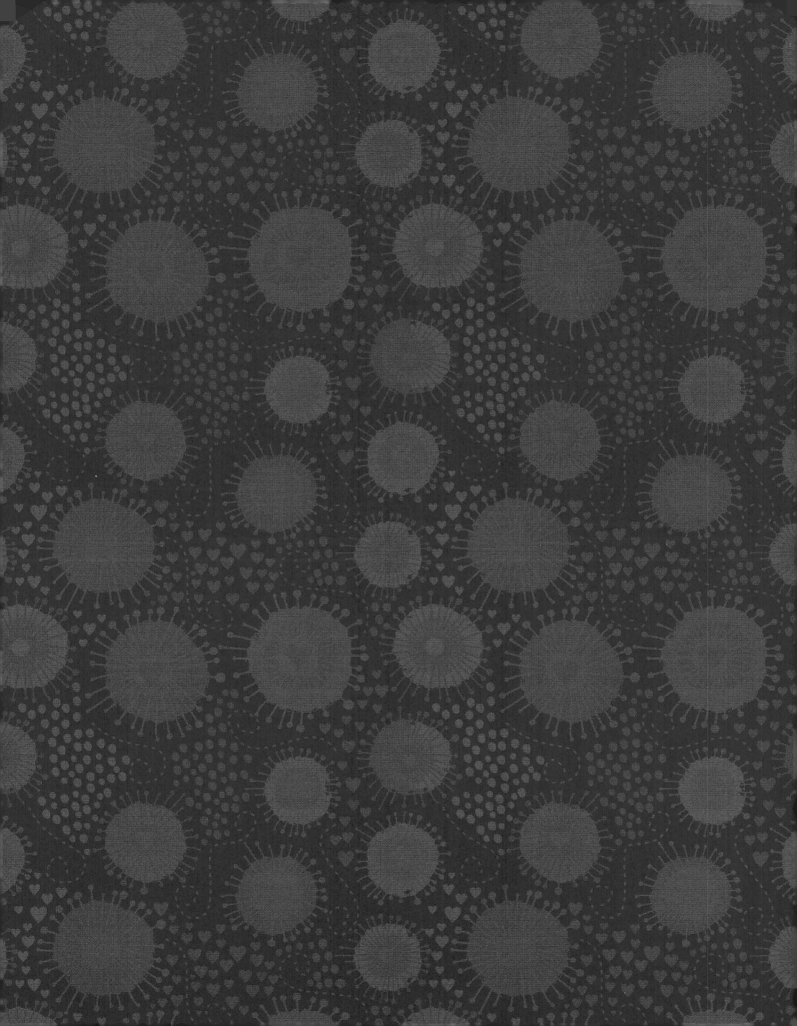

I'M ON THAT NEW DIET WHERE YOU EAT EVERYTHING AND HOPE FOR A MIRACLE.

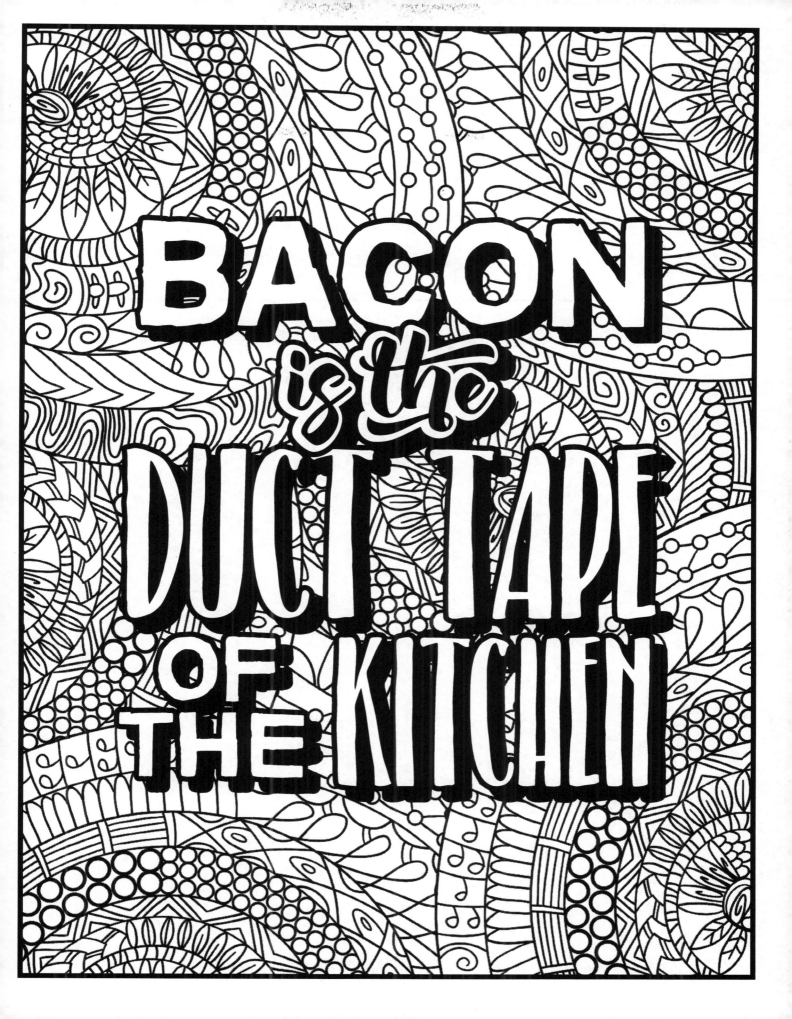

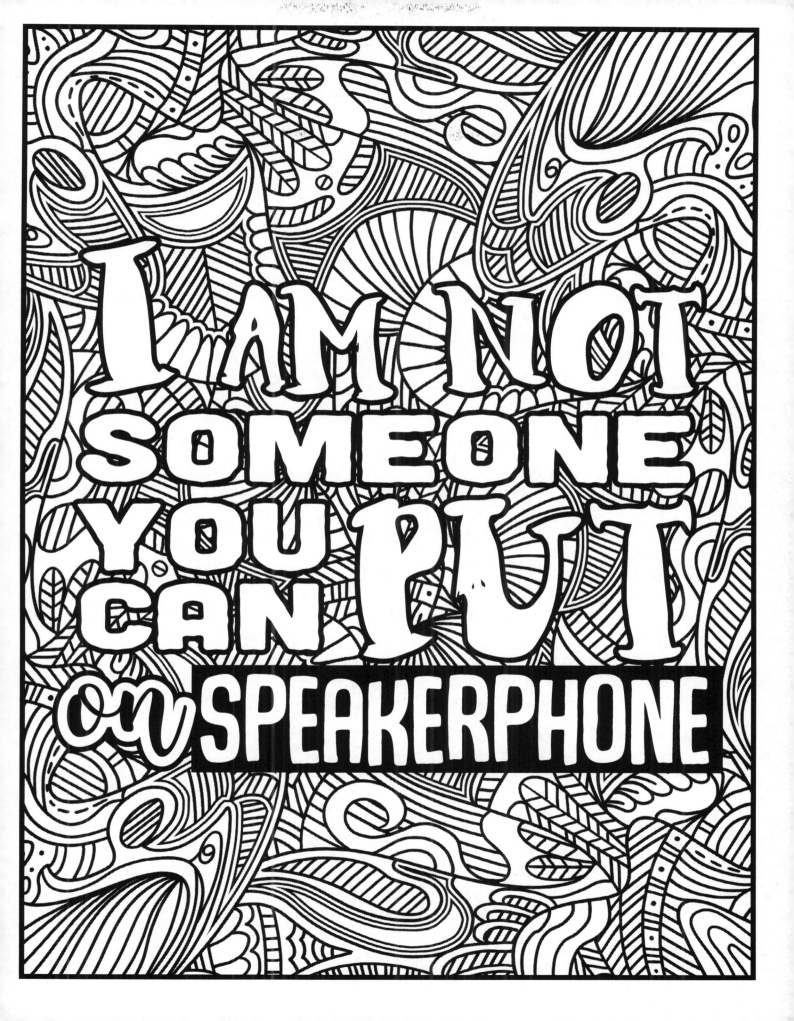

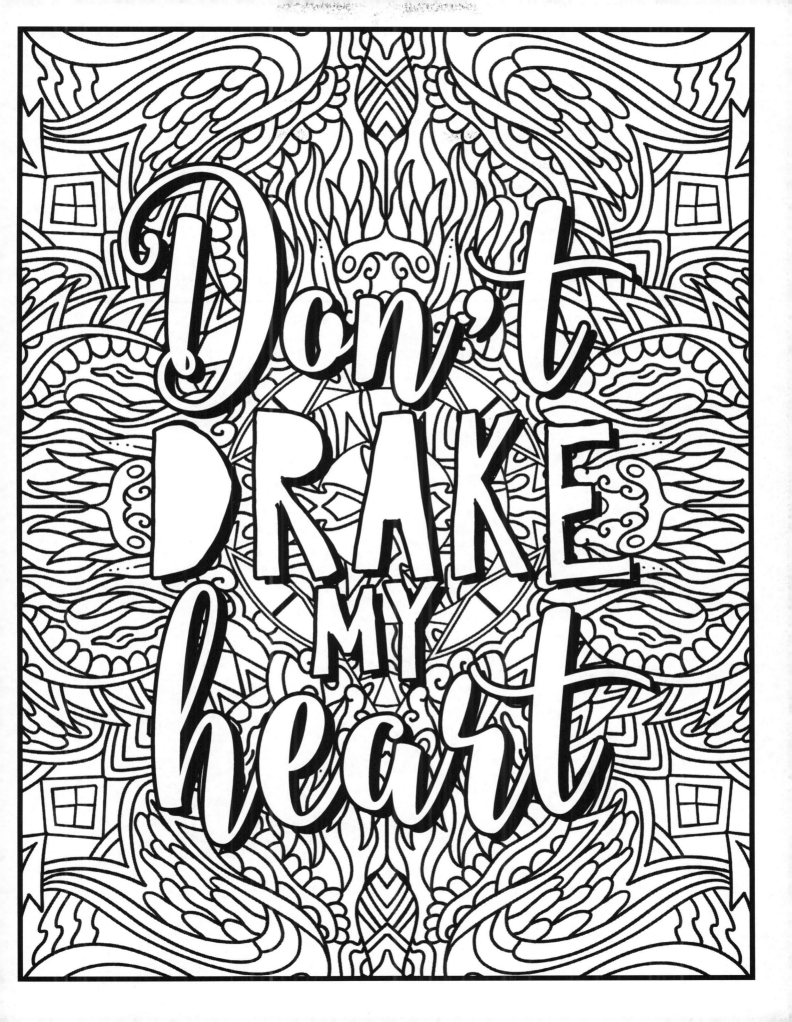

BE SURE TO FOLLOW US
ON SOCIAL MEDIA FOR THE
LATEST NEWS, SNEAK
PEEKS, & GIVEAWAYS

:camera: @PapeterieBleu

:facebook: Papeterie Bleu

:twitter: @PapeterieBleu

ADD YOURSELF TO OUR MONTHLY
NEWSLETTER FOR FREE DIGITAL
DOWNLOADS AND DISCOUNT CODES

www.papeteriebleu.com/newsletter

CHECK OUT OUR OTHER BOOKS!

www.papateriebleu.com

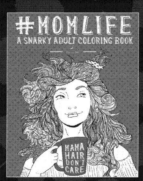

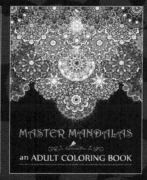

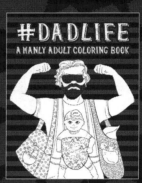

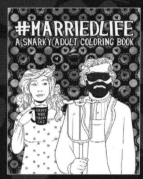

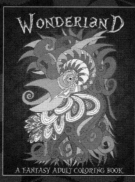

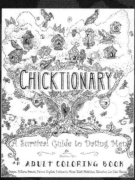

CHECK OUT OUR OTHER BOOKS!

www.papeteriebleu.com

CHECK OUT OUR OTHER BOOKS!

www.papeteriebleu.com

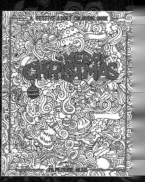

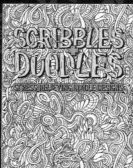

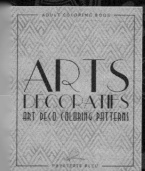

Made in the USA
Columbia, SC
12 June 2018